CW01665598

The Heart of Christmas

Daily reflections for Advent

Chris Morley

kevin mayhew

kevin mayhew

First published in Great Britain in 2009 by Kevin Mayhew Ltd
Buxhall, Stowmarket, Suffolk IP14 3BW
Tel: +44 (0) 1449 737978 Fax: +44 (0) 1449 737834
E-mail: info@kevinmayhewltd.com

www.kevinmayhew.com

9 8 7 6 5 4 3 2 1 0

ISBN 978 1 84867 205 5
Catalogue No. 1501196

Cover design by Rob Mortonson
Design and layout by Chris Coe
Edited by Alison Evans

Printed and bound in Great Britain

Contents

To my father, Peter Morley, who was a constant source of encouragement and inspiration.

About the author

Chris Morley has recently retired after nearly 40 years as a Methodist Minister. He worked mainly in churches in London and also has experience of prison and school chaplaincy. He first started writing short daily reflections on an internet site and has subsequently become a regular contributor to the 'Pause for Thought' slot on Terry Wogan's Radio 2 Breakfast Show.

Preface

Human behaviour is a rich source of delight, analysis and humour. Most of our casual conversation is spent talking about it. Jesus often used examples of it to illustrate something he wanted to say. In the behaviour of those who feature in his parables, he found pictures which opened up to those who listened to him, a deeper understanding of God.

Today's world is no less rich in such similes. I enjoy, especially, finding quirky examples of human behaviour which offer ways into reflecting on God and on my response to him. I've found as I use these, that I'm also led into thinking about myself and what's going on inside me.

This little book offers some of these reflections for use during Advent. It's good in these often busy weeks before Christmas, to remind ourselves what it means that God embraced humanity. One certain result of that birth in Bethlehem, is that our understanding of God and of what it is to be human, was hugely enlarged. I want this book to help its readers achieve growth in that same understanding.

Each day's reflection is followed by some things to think about. Some of these won't ring bells with you at all; there may be others which do strike a chord and which you may feel your mind coming back to, until a new insight emerges from your subconscious and you receive it as a gift from God.

Two things are important about these suggestions. One is that you see them as your servant not your master! The other is that you engage with them as part of your ongoing conversation with God. I haven't, as I might have done, offered a prayer to sum up each day's reflection. This is partly because no two people's response will be the same and I don't want to prejudge the direction your thoughts might go. But it's mainly because I hope you will consciously open yourself to God's presence as you work with the suggestions that appeal to you, and invite contributions to your internal debate, not just from the different parts of yourself, but also from the Spirit of God that is within you. Such a use of the suggestions won't be like a formal prayer but will be praying.

I'm grateful to many people for their encouragement as I've worked on these reflections. John Gibbon, Annette O'Connor Boyd and Wendy Spray all kindly made comments on my original script which improved it. I'm particularly grateful to my wife, Myriel, who encouraged me to think I could write. Conversations with her form the basis of many of the ideas here.

Chris Morley

Week one

Judging

Advent Sunday

Rick Pyburn was sick and tired of motorists speeding past his home in a quiet village. He and his neighbours had fun standing in a conspicuous place holding hand-held speed detectors loaned from the police, but when they weren't there, drivers simply reverted to their former speeds.

Then, one day, Rick got an idea. With the help of a local sign company, he used plywood to build a two-dimensional image of a police car. He set up the decoy in some bushes next to his home. 'With that just in view of the road, the transformation was amazing,' he said. 'The traffic, even when it wasn't breaking the limit, slowed immediately.'

Many Advent Sunday readings contain admonitions that we should check on our lifestyle and behaviour, because a time of judgement is approaching. The signs are there, they warn us, that the Son of Man will soon appear and woe betide us if we're caught unprepared. Like the drivers through Rick Pyburn's village, our initial reaction might be to pull up our socks. These days, though, it's harder to take the danger of that kind of judgement seriously, because so many generations have passed without any sign of it.

Perhaps more effective as an incentive than external threats, is an inner longing for a different kind of life. The picture more likely to stimulate us is not one of God the authority figure warning of punishment, but one of Jesus showing us what human life at its best can be like. Advent can be a useful time for reflection on what motivates us, and what changes in our lives or attitudes might make us more fulfilled and effective human beings. In that process, the baby in the manger is a much more effective agent for change than a plywood cut out or signs in the heavens.

Read God has destined us, not to receive his anger, but to obtain liberation through our Lord Jesus Christ.
(1 Thessalonians 5:9)

Rejoice that God didn't just tell us how to live; in Jesus' life, he showed us.

Reflect What changes would I most like to make in my life?

Remember just wanting to be different is sufficient to give God something to work with.

Resolve to be open this Advent to any changes God might want me to make.

Monday

The National Trust once launched a campaign to find the country's ugliest vegetable. Gardeners were encouraged to submit anything 'from two-legged carrots to corkscrew runner beans'. Entrants were given a year's notice to produce something ugly. 'We want to counter a trend among retailers for stocking perfect-looking fruit and vegetables, regardless of its taste,' said a National Trust representative.

Most gardeners preparing produce for a show would want to enter what looked best. Indeed, most of us want our lives and what we do with them to look as near to perfect as possible. This is the path, we might feel, towards gaining people's respect and developing self-esteem.

Jesus did teach that one way of judging people is by their 'fruits' but that, at a deeper level, it is the inner person God's interested in, not what they have or have not done. And even when what's inside is less than appealing, God doesn't turn his back on anyone. The elder son in one of Jesus' stories laid claim to recognition because of his thorough and committed work on the farm. But it was the younger who had prodigally spent his inheritance for whom a banquet was thrown, in spite of his ugly and destructive behaviour.

Many of us feel an inner pressure to make everything we do, and indeed ourselves, perfect. But we're also aware how unrealistic that is and know that that isn't what God's most interested in. In fact, we can be ugly both inside and out and God will still be glad he created us. So if we fall short of what we expect of ourselves, we shouldn't judge ourselves failures in God's eyes, or in our own.

Read The Pharisees said of Jesus: This fellow welcomes sinners and eats with them. *(Luke 15:2)*

Rejoice that God isn't put off even when I seem to be consistently failing.

Reflect Am I too concerned about doing well in any of my current activities?

Remember that God gives me permission to stop trying to be perfect.

Resolve not to lower my standards but to be more relaxed about achieving them.

Tuesday

On one occasion, in Cornwall, a parking warden clamped a van belonging to a dead man and then refused to waive the £350 release fee. In Kristiansand, on Norway's southern tip, a motorist unable to move because of rush hour traffic got a parking ticket. The officials involved would clearly have benefited from more training – perhaps the little-known BTEC qualification for 'immobilisation operatives'. Described as a course to assist clampers and parking wardens with communication skills and conflict resolution, let's hope it also equips them to make less stupid decisions!

It's not only parking wardens who do stupid things; and a thirty-hour training course wouldn't make much difference to our tendency to make silly mistakes or behave foolishly. Careless speech or clumsy behaviour can leave us feeling very red in the face, even when only we know about it.

Occasionally, embarrassment is the only appropriate response. But often there is a reason why we have done or said something stupid. It may be a sign that we are overtired, or that we are feeling threatened, or that something not yet identified is making us uncomfortable. It's sensible in such circumstances not to berate ourselves, but to make careful judgements about why we might have behaved like that. We can make something creative out of a faux pas if we pause to reflect on why this normally sensible person suddenly does something silly; and then do something about it.

Read You discern my thoughts from far away ...Even before a word is on my tongue, O Lord, you know it completely. *(Psalm 139:2, 4)*

Rejoice that God's response to our mistakes is unfailingly forgiving.

Reflect What underlying cause can I spot for any recent uncharacteristic behaviour?

Remember that God is there to help us when we're trying to understand ourselves.

Resolve to practice the art of seeking out the hidden motivations which drive my behaviour.

Wednesday

Dutch TV company, Endemol, were out to break their own Guinness World Record of 3,992,397 falling dominoes. They had worked for weeks setting up more than 4 million dominoes when a sparrow flew in and knocked over 23,000 of them. The common house sparrow, a species on the national endangered list, was chased into a corner and shot by an exterminator with an air rifle. An Endemol representative defended the action: 'More than 100 people from 12 countries had worked for more than a month setting them up. It was very frustrating'.

The sparrow posed a threat to Endemol's project. Indeed, human plans and good intentions are often threatened and undermined. Sometimes it's other people whose selfishness or disturbed behaviour interrupts otherwise previously peaceful lives. Sometimes it's more inside ourselves – we are aware in our own lives of doing or saying things which often seem to emerge unbidden from our subconscious, but which cause hurt to others or are destructive of our best endeavours. Then, looking back on how we behaved, we're often angry with ourselves for being or acting like that and fearful because we don't know how to stop it happening again.

God doesn't deal with such human failings in the way Endemol dealt with the sparrow. Nor is his main response the frustration we often feel with ourselves.

He may judge much of our behaviour to be damaging but he doesn't express his disappointment by acting impetuously. Instead, he comes to share in the human struggle to deal with our destructive behaviour, and on the Cross became its victim.

When we're conscious of something inside us that's undermining our lives and our loving, remembering that God has come to help us deal with it, is more likely to engender change than just getting frustrated.

Read I do not understand my own actions . . . I do not do the good I want, but the evil I do not want is what I do . . . Who will rescue me . . . ? *(Romans 7:15, 19, 24)*

Rejoice that Jesus came to take our human self-destructiveness in hand.

Reflect Am I sometimes too hard on myself?

Remember that I am loved by God in spite of myself.

Resolve to seek God's help if I feel any of my behaviour is damaging me or someone else.

Thursday

Australian, John Fleming, worked for a company that makes road signs. Among them are those warning motorists about kangaroos of which there are more than 57 million in the country. They account for more than 70 per cent of animal-related accidents. Sadly for Mr Fleming's motorbike, and for the kangaroo, he ran into one of them recently. 'I was riding my motorbike with my mate when the kangaroo jumped straight into it,' he told Australia's *Herald Sun* newspaper. 'The guys from work sent me a get well card – it showed a kangaroo warning sign.'

It seems as though spending all day surrounded by warnings about kangaroos is no protection from them. The publicity surrounding Mr Fleming's experience was probably far more effective in preventing future accidents than warning signs. It's unlikely that those who heard what happened to him, will, for a while anyway, need road signs to remind them how dangerous kangaroos can be.

The prophets, whose words are recorded in the Old Testament, were constantly challenging the people of Israel to take seriously the consequences of their behaviour. Yet they seemed incapable of living their lives in a way even remotely resembling what God wanted from them. God's choice to come in Jesus seemed to be saying: if warning signs won't persuade you, perhaps seeing the effects of your refusal to listen to me in the experience of an innocent man, might be more convincing.

When we do what we shouldn't or fail to do what we should, we don't generally need to be told. Like Mr Fleming, we know perfectly well what's sensible and right. What we need is help to change. Seeing on the Cross the effects of our human refusal to listen to God and Jesus' forgiving response, is more likely to achieve that than any number of warnings.

Read Look and see if there is any sorrow like my sorrow. *(Lamentations 1:12)*

Rejoice that Jesus never strayed from God's ways.

Reflect Can I identify any consequences in my life of my failure to live God's way?

Remember Jesus never criticised people for failing to achieve high standards, only for pretending that they had.

Resolve to keep in my mind the thought of God's forgiving love expressed on the Cross.

Friday

One year, a hotel chain offered couples named Mary and Joseph a free night's stay over Christmas. Travelodge said it was trying to make up for the hotel industry not having any rooms left on that first Christmas Eve. The offer came with just one proviso – to claim their free night's stay, Marys and Josephs had to prove their identity. That of course was why the original Mary and Joseph travelled to Bethlehem. They had to register in the town Joseph's family came from. If they weren't counted there, then as far as the government of the time was concerned, they didn't exist.

Many people feel they don't count: homeless people, those rejected by their families or those they thought loved them, those who do menial jobs, are unemployed or mentally ill. Then there are those who don't quite fit in socially. 'I just hope our Marys and Josephs don't bring their donkey,' said a Travelodge representative. We all know people whose presence creates a slight social awkwardness.

The default response to people like this is avoidance. It's more comfortable to make the same judgement about them as everyone else. But it would be more loving if we were to imagine, or even find out, what lies behind their situation. It's likely then, that we'd want to help them feel they did count, and even if we didn't entirely sympathise with them, somehow to make them feel less excluded. The innkeeper who found space for the pregnant woman and her husband is a good role model for us all.

Read See [says the Lord], I will bring them home . . . the blind and the lame, expectant mothers and women in labour; a great throng. *(Jeremiah 31:8)*

Rejoice that no one is excluded from God's care.

Reflect Is there anything more I could do for those on the fringes of society who need support?

Remember if opening myself to someone else's situation feels frightening, I can be sure of God's backing.

Resolve to notice people who are feeling sidelined and, if they appear to want to, find ways of drawing them in.

Saturday

When Oliver Cromwell became Lord Protector of England in 1653, people were not allowed to celebrate Christmas. It had become a holiday of celebration and enjoyment but Cromwell and his fellow Protestant Parliamentarians wanted it returned to a religious celebration, where people thought about the birth of Jesus rather than ate and drank too much. In London, soldiers were ordered to go round the streets and take, by force if necessary, food being prepared for a Christmas celebration. The smell of a goose being cooked could only bring trouble. Traditional Christmas decorations like holly were banned.

People with strong views about religion still try and impose those views on others. Sadly, some even use force to do so. But there's an intolerance that doesn't include violence too. Religious people sometimes criticise those who have no faith. Those whose outlook is entirely secular sometimes revile believers. Such judgemental approaches not only create hurt – they also prevent creative dialogue.

When they do it with open-mindedness, the variety of different ways in which people articulate their spirituality can be a source of delight. We might use the proximity of Christmas to encourage conversations about why we believe what we do, or for less personal exchanges, of differing opinions on religion. Anything like Cromwell's attempt to take the secularism out of

Christmas would be a non-starter today as then, but we could perhaps play our part in putting the religion back into it.

Read Paul said: 'Athenians, I see how extremely religious you are in every way . . . I found among [you] an altar with the inscription, "To an unknown God"'. *(Acts 17:22, 23)*

Rejoice in the way other people's spiritual understanding has helped me develop my own.

Reflect Does the secular celebration of Christmas add anything to my spiritual experience of it?

Remember Jesus was often critical of people for being too 'religious'.

Resolve to have a conversation on what life's about with someone who might feel differently from me.

Week two

Waiting

Second Sunday in Advent

To celebrate their seventieth anniversary, the British Council asked 40,000 people in 102 non-English speaking countries, their favourite English word. Lollipop (42), flip-flop (59), hen night (70), hiccup (63), hodgepodge (64), and whoops (56) were among the top seventy. Their appeal was how they sounded. But the top ten were: mother, passion, smile, love, eternity, fantastic, destiny, freedom, liberty and tranquillity. Here it's clearly the meaning that counts. Those surveyed were expressing what they hoped for from life.

It's valuable, occasionally, to ask ourselves what we want most. Sometimes we'll find we already have it and can be grateful. Sometimes by asking the question, we discover or remember a longing which had got buried in the busyness of life. Often we may find in something we read or hear that our deepest desires are expressed in a way we could never have discovered for ourselves, because often we just can't find the words to describe what we most deeply want. There's something there, experienced perhaps, in a niggling dissatisfaction with how things are, but we can't articulate it. We feel that if we could find a way to express it, even to ourselves, we would be much nearer knowing how to start working for it.

For long years of waiting, the people of Israel wanted more from God. Their prophets were sometimes effective in putting their longings into words. Often the people got impatient, going after goals which they thought would satisfy but didn't. Part of God's purpose in becoming human was to show them a complete expression of the rich relationship between God and his people, which alone would bring them the sense of fulfilment they sought.

For us too, our deepest longings find expression in the Word made flesh. Jesus' life speaks not only of how life might be, but reveals how we might set about discovering it.

Read Peter said to Jesus: 'You have the words of eternal life'. *(John 6:68)*

Rejoice that God knows what I most deeply need, even if I don't, and has the power to give it.

Reflect What words appeal most to me?

Remember to listen for the words God might be putting into my head.

Resolve to pay attention to 'niggling dissatisfaction' and ask what it might be telling me.

Monday

Each May, 120 of the rich and famous do a 3000 mile drive. In their Ferraris, Lamborghinis, Rolls Royces, vintage Aston Martins or Bentleys, celebrities of all sorts pay a minimum of £20,000 for the eight-day event (£60,000 when it was San Francisco to Beijing in Olympics year). It's partly an excuse for a hectic round of parties, and attempts to turn Gumball 3000 into a race are frowned upon. But competition between the drivers of these fast, big-engined cars is inevitable; no one worries though, if the cost of fines for speeding mounts – it's worth it to live life in the fast lane for a week.

There is another view of life. Carl Honoré has started a movement he calls 'In Praise of Slow'. He's in touch with groups throughout the world trying to encourage us all to go slower. There is, for example, The Sloth Club in Japan and The Society for the Deceleration of Time.

Many of us these days, rush through life. Often the first thing we do on waking is to look at the clock, and we keep our eye on timepieces of one sort or another throughout the day. Many of us keep mental lists of what needs to be done and feel anxious if we 'get behind'. This time of year is notorious for hectic and constant activity.

The New Testament's word for this approach to time is 'chronos'. But more important than clock time are times of particular significance or 'kairos' moments, times when God reveals himself in large or small ways. The most important of these is the coming of Jesus. Not being so anxious about chronos will make us more ready to spot a kairos. 'In Praise of Slow' is catching on fast, so for all sorts of reasons we'd better hurry up and start slowing down!

Read Be still and know that I am God. *(Psalm 46:10)*

Rejoice in those times when the timing of an event or experience has felt just right.

Reflect What are the things I usually try to do too fast?

Remember there are things I can choose not to do today.

Resolve to take pride today in doing something really slowly.

Tuesday

In the early days of digital television, the BBC needed an advertising gimmick. So, for an experimental week, we had *Pet TV*. For example: clips of rolling snooker balls, flying frisbees, and feline cartoon characters offered a cat, weary after a busy day, something to relax to and a purrfect antidote to life's stresses.

There was apparently a scientific side to the experiment. The BBC said they wanted feedback from owners about what sounds and images their pets responded to. Did they respond to dogs barking or wolves howling or parrots talking? Were fish attracted by the sound of running water, or cats, by the sight of fish swimming in a tank?

But there was realism about the BBC's publicity: 'If your pet shows no interest, don't force it to watch – it might not be in the right mood' – they're right, most goldfish have better things to do than put their tails up and swish on the TV for a bit of R & R.

We all have different ways of relaxing. Its importance is enshrined in the Ten Commandments, where we're reminded that God chose to 'rest' after the creation. The word used for rest in the Hebrew literally means 'getting your soul back'. Probably most of our leisure time is spent in activity – we might put our feet up for a while, but before long we're restless to be engaged in something more specific.

But the kind of relaxation which revives our souls,

helps us rediscover who we are, is more likely to be passive than active. Animals that resist their owners' pressure to do something useful while they're relaxing, may have a point. Sometimes doing nothing may have a value all of its own.

Read My presence will go with you and I will give you rest. *(Exodus 33:14)*

Rejoice in the opportunities I have, to take breaks from my normal routine.

Reflect Have I got the balance right between work and rest?

Remember in pressured periods of my life, even taking a brief moment to recall God's presence is refreshing.

Resolve to check that the ways I choose to relax, do refresh me.

Wednesday

Even when she was in her nineties, Jessie Smart knitted more than a hundred scarves every year. They were sold at the Christmas fayre at her care home and she's raised hundreds of pounds. Mrs Smart said she didn't like sitting doing nothing; she preferred to do something active that would benefit others.

Many of us find sitting doing nothing, difficult. That's why some kinds of waiting can be so irritating if you haven't gone prepared with some activity to fill the time. Even the sitting still, normally associated with praying, can be a challenge. We like to be doing something. So maybe, when it comes to that 'waiting on God' which is an important part of prayer, the answer is to find something physical we can do that will still leave our minds free to be open to God.

An Archbishop in the Russian Orthodox Church, the late Anthony Bloom, once offered this advice. He told a woman who came seeking a way to sense God's presence, that she was to tidy her room so that nothing in it would distract her, sit in a corner of it, and knit something for which she didn't need a pattern. She reported back that the activity she'd been mindlessly engaged in, had enabled her to be still in every other way, that she felt as though she was knitting 'before the face of God' and that she'd begun to feel aware of a rich and dense silence which was also a presence.

We shall be more ready to celebrate the coming of

God at Christmas if we wait expectantly for it throughout the year. One way of doing this is to take time to be still. If, as we try to do that, the need to be active feels overwhelming, finding ways of mindlessly occupying our bodies can help. Such waiting often remains just that, but occasionally, such attentiveness to God is rewarded.

Read When you pray, go into your room and shut the door and pray to your Father who . . . will reward you. *(Matthew 6:6)*

Rejoice in God's eagerness to come to us.

Reflect What mindless activity might keep my body happy while my soul seeks stillness?

Remember if we can't keep still, God will find another way to relate to us.

Resolve to sit still for a while today.

Thursday

Wang Guiying was afraid to marry when she was young but at the age of 107, she decided to look for her first husband. She worked on the land till she was 74 but when, at 102, she broke her leg, she began to worry about becoming a burden to her ageing nieces and nephews. She told the *Chongqing Commercial Times* that she hoped to find a fellow centenarian so they would have something to talk about.

She'd been put off marriage by the childhood sight of her uncles and other men scolding and beating their wives and often found her aunt crying in the woodshed after an attack. 'All the married people around there lived like that. Getting married was too frightening,' she said. Eventually she changed her mind but had she missed the boat?

Our experience of life can sometimes make us cautious. As we see the difficulties other people face and we struggle with our own, the world can sometimes feel a hostile place and we become reluctant to take any risks that aren't strictly necessary. If we become conscious of changes that might make our lives more satisfying, we're tempted to put off making them until we feel more secure or the change less risky.

God's coming in Jesus, tells us he wants to share with us in these kinds of decision. He wants to be part of the process of deciding which changes are appropriate and which, merely attractive – the right ones are often a gift from him anyway – and he won't leave us alone if we step boldly into a different future. But in the end it must be our decision to take the leap. There comes a point, in the small decisions in life and in the more significant ones, when going on waiting is no longer appropriate. Wait too long and the moment may have passed.

Read After waiting patiently, Abraham received what was promised. *(Hebrews 6:15)*

Rejoice in any experience of making a change in my life that proved beneficial.

Reflect Is there anything I'm putting off at the moment because I'm worried where it might lead?

Remember my fearfulness may mean I let opportunities go, but God won't let go of me.

Resolve to let God lead me, whether it's into patient waiting or decisive action.

Friday

It took Graham Parker 26 years to solve the puzzle of the Rubik's Cube. He bought the toy in 1983 when millions were intrigued by the challenge it set to get coloured shapes round a cube in the right order. He was 19 then, breakfast TV was a novelty and music CDs were in the shops for the first time. 'I cannot tell you what a relief it was to finally solve it,' he said. 'It felt as though it had taken over my life. I would lie awake at night thinking about it, I've had wrist problems from spending hours on it but it was all worth it. When the last bit clicked into place and each face was a solid colour, I wept.'

Being unable to sleep for thinking is a common human experience. Whether it's an upsetting situation we're in, concern over someone we care about, something we're planning or a relationship that's making us anxious, we can't get it out of our heads and though few of these worries last 26 years, the relief when the waiting is over and the situation is resolved can sometimes make us weep.

It's easy to let obsessions such as this take over our lives. But like Graham Parker, though he may not have realised it, we have a choice. We don't have to allow them to take hold of us so overwhelmingly. Letting go is no easy matter. One way is to have a more comfortable topic ready to replace it with, whenever the painful subject comes into our minds. More effective is being able to share the burden with someone – a friend perhaps. Talking about it can release some of the pressure that builds up inside us. The baby born in the stable offers to be such a friend. Telling him about it and letting him carry the burden may not resolve the situation, but the relief it brings can also make us want to weep.

Read Cast your burden on the Lord and he will sustain you. *(Psalm 55:22)*

Rejoice in friends with whom I share 'carrying each other's burdens'.

Reflect Am I obsessive about anything?

Remember when I do lie awake worrying, God's there too.

Resolve to share something that's worrying me with someone I can trust.

Saturday

When John Cage, the twentieth-century composer, said that his composition Organ^2/ASLSP should be played 'as slow as possible' he may not have meant that its performance should be spread over 639 years. But this is how a group of German music experts in the German town of Halberstadt have interpreted his instructions.

Their performance, on a specially built organ in which keys are held down by weights, began on 5 September, 2001. It started with eighteen months of silence. The first notes were played on 5 February 2003. New notes or chords are always added on the fifth day of a month but the frequency varies. For example, the change in February 2009 was only three months after the previous one but the one following it is sixteen months later.

Life often seems to consist of a series of deadlines which crowd mercilessly upon us. In situations like that, such an unhurried approach to life sounds attractive. It helps to have a longer perspective, to view our tasks as part of a much longer-term project. This, of course, is God's perspective and, if we allow it, God is also the composer, enabling and encouraging identifiable changes in our lives at what appear to us to be purely random intervals. When we trust God to do that, we can approach our lives in a less frenetic way, and perhaps ultimately see a pattern which is missed if we are only conscious of immediate pressures. The individual chords which make up our lives today may not always make sense out of context, but we trust they are part of a sustained and longer-term harmony.

Read In your book were written . . . the days that were formed for me, when as yet there was none of them. *(Psalm 139:16)*

Rejoice that I'm free to make my own choices and God will work even with my wrong decisions.

Reflect Can I identify any examples in my life of God's timing being just right?

Remember that it's being responsive to God's promptings, not understanding them, that's important.

Resolve to trust in God's knowledge of what's best for me and his ability to make it happen.

Week three

Saving

Third Sunday in Advent

A giant white radish broke through asphalt to grow fruitfully on a road in the Japanese town of Aioi. Local residents nicknamed the vegetable 'Gutsy Radish'. Asked why the radish had so many fans, a town spokesman said: 'People discouraged by tough times are cheered by its tenacity and strong will to live.'

So imagine the outrage when the radish was decapitated by an unknown assailant. In fact, so great was the furore, that the culprit the next day replaced the top half of the radish near the site where it had been growing. The repentant attacker had placed it in water to try to keep it alive and in the hope it might yet flower again.

There are a number of possible reasons why we might come to regret an action we've taken or something we said. One is the realisation, like the one experienced by the radish-slayer, of the effect we've had on others. Another is an internal awareness of the wrongness of the action, perhaps one that was already there before it was done but which we chose to ignore. Then there's that sinking feeling that comes when a friend, even if ever so gently, points out a way we've let ourselves down without realising it.

John the Baptist's admonitions were far from gentle but he seems to have struck a chord with his contemporaries. He had no suggestions to make about how to make restitution – indeed in the majority of situations, attempts to undo or make up for what's been done are as futile as replacing the radish. He recommended repentance, expressing regret and determining to behave differently in future, and promised one would come whose life and work would transform the way we view our wrongdoing.

Read John the Baptist proclaimed: 'Repent, for the kingdom of God has come near'. *(Matthew 3:2)*

Rejoice that God doesn't leave us with a sense of having failed, but comes to offer us a new way forward.

Reflect Are there any actions or words I'm still trying to make up for, when really all I can do is to express regret and behave differently in the future?

Remember other people are sometimes more forgiving of us than we are of ourselves.

Resolve to be generous in offering my apologies . . . and in receiving them.

Monday

Roadworks which cause long diversions can cause frustration, particularly at this time of year. In Shepherd's Bush, West London, on one occasion, 300 yards of roadworks led drivers to be taken over fly-overs along the North Circular, through the perpetual gridlock of Hanger Lane and back through industrial estates – 12 miles in all. 'It is a lengthy diversion,' said a representative of Transport for London, 'but we would not be behaving sensibly if we sent this traffic down roads which could not cope.'

Sometimes, as we reflect on our lives, we feel we've gone a long way round to get to where we are now. Perhaps it was because we couldn't see the direct route at the time; perhaps we weren't even sure where we wanted to get to. We just muddled through doing what seemed best or simply letting events lead us.

The Christmas story describes the travellers from the east as having been guided by a star. They were diverted from the most direct route and went via Herod's palace but in the end they arrived safely at their destination.

Maybe just now we're not aware of having arrived anywhere. We're not sure where we're going. But sometimes, looking back, what seemed frustrating diversions at the time, turned out to be significant in bringing us to where we are now. Perhaps the route, though long, had its compensations as new discoveries were made on the way; or delay was required so that the timing of our arrival was right; or going the way we did avoided experiences we couldn't have coped with. The journey doesn't seem so long if we feel we can trust the creators of the diversion to get us to the right place in the end.

Read In your unfailing love you will lead the people you have redeemed.
(Exodus 15:13)

Rejoice in those times when I've been conscious of God leading me.

Reflect Am I willing to let God guide me . . . or do I feel I always know the best route?

Remember just because I don't know where I'm going, it doesn't mean God doesn't.

Resolve to look out, when I'm not where I want to be, for good reasons for being where I am.

Tuesday

Recently, an unusual kind of present apparently became fashionable. 'Demand is up about 25 percent,' reported a plastic surgeon one Christmas. 'I am operating from morning to night. People want to be able to stand under the Christmas tree with their new car, new sofa and new lips or breasts.'

Much of what happens at Christmas is traditional. Part of the point is that it doesn't change. But the increasing number of lifts, tucks and implants being given as presents by those who can afford it, suggests that for some at least, there is a desire to be different.

The dissatisfaction some feel with how they look reflects a sense of unease experienced by many more of us about how we are or what we're doing. We'd like to stand under the Christmas tree as new people, proud of who we are, at peace with ourselves and those around us because the less attractive parts of our personalities and lives have been ironed out.

A Christmas song says: 'There's a new world beginning from tonight.' What sets it going is the new insight into God's love brought by Jesus' birth. God loves us enough to come and share in the struggles and joys of being human. Not only that, but he doesn't wait for us to be worthy to receive him – he comes to us as we are. We don't need to change to be loved. We can stand tall, approaching this Christmas with that new confidence and peace for which we long, not because the parts of us we don't like have been surgically removed, but because we know that they, like the rest of us, are loved.

Read God shows his love for us in that while we were yet sinners, Christ died for us. *(Romans 5:8)*

Rejoice in the encouragement God gives me to accept myself as I am.

Reflect What aspects of my life and myself give me pleasure?

Remember putting pressure on myself to be different can be counter-productive.

Resolve to remind myself regularly that God loves me.

Wednesday

A few years ago, Brad Meltzer wrote a short series of comic books and they were published by the firm that features Superman, Batman, Wonder Woman and many other well-known heroes. The comic book world was thrown into turmoil because in these stories, Batman is in despair, Superman is questioning his abilities and Wonder Woman has lost her wonder. The story began with a brutal murder for which they all felt partly to blame. Superman even shed a tear. Guilt, grief and remorse didn't seem consistent with the usually heroic behaviour of these characters, and there was concern among fans about these long-invincible characters experiencing such dramatic identity crises.

Self-doubt and distress in one of our heroes or heroines can be unsettling. Seeing even them struggle with pain or worries reminds us how potentially destructive such feelings can be – if they have this effect on them, how will I manage? Part of us would prefer the reassurance of someone unshakeable to lean on. But another part finds strength in recognising that all human beings experience such emotions and from seeing the heroic way they often deal with them.

In the birth of Jesus, God offered the world a hero about whose inner life we know virtually nothing. But he did display sadness, disappointment and inner turmoil. He was far from the invulnerable and invincible hero the popular imagination often seeks.

Brad Meltzer said he was trying to give these characters a new 'human' side. Jesus' life affirms the human side of God. Being tested, facing struggle and frailty, were all part of his life as they are part of ours. A hero who helps us acknowledge our human weakness will be much more helpful than one who pretends that our salvation is in invincibility.

Read When I am weak, then I am strong.
(2 Corinthians 12:10)

Rejoice in those whose way of dealing with struggles in their life has inspired me.

Reflect Am I leaning on anyone?

Remember God wants me to lean on him.

Resolve to find people's vulnerability inspiring, as well as their strength.

Thursday

The memorial service for Ginny, a Schnauzer-Siberian Husky, was attended by some 300 cats. Ginny died, aged 17, after a long career as a one-dog rescue party for cats on Long Island's south shore. Cat lover, Philip Gonzalez, used to take the dog out every night to feed stray cats in the area, and over the years, Ginny saved hundreds of cats who were abandoned, injured or in harm's way. She once ignored the cuts on her paws as she dug through a box full of broken glass to find an injured cat inside. On another occasion, she threw herself against a vertical pipe at a construction site to topple it and reveal the kittens trapped inside.

Dogs are renowned for their loyalty to their human owners but such concern for another animal species is remarkable. In human beings too, care for our own families and those like us comes naturally, but people whose lifestyle or assumptions are totally unlike ours or who have a very different cultural background, present more of a challenge. It's when care is offered across those kinds of boundaries that a deeper humanity is revealed.

Jesus' life was distinguished by such caring. His loving for people whom Jewish society thought of as beyond the pale – prostitutes, tax collectors, non-Jews – crossed boundaries and challenges us to check again whether our loving extends to people whose difference from us might deter us.

Indeed, the very existence of Jesus reveals how God too crosses that kind of boundary. Without his coming, what's human and what's divine would have continued to seem very far apart. But God wanted to save us from that narrow-mindedness which limits our capacity to love. He showed the way in Jesus when he embraced our humanity with his divinity.

Read He is our peace . . . he has broken down the dividing wall of hostility.
(Ephesians 2:14)

Rejoice that God's not put off loving me when I'm being 'all too human'.

Reflect Is there anyone – or any group of people – I'm not reaching out to because I'm put off by their difference?

Remember there's much to be learnt from loving people who initially seem very different from me.

Resolve to take the next opportunity I have to cross a social barrier.

Friday

At a secret summit of Santas, new guidelines were agreed. Father Christmas must have a bushy white beard no more than six inches long and a girth no greater than 48 inches and no less than 46 inches. 'We are trying to eradicate shoddy Santas,' said a spokesperson from the Ministry of Fun agency which fills 500 Santa positions a year. 'I even saw a Santa last year wearing trainers.' The hope is that under the new directives, every Santa's grotto will be adorned by a neatly presented Santa and a properly resonant 'Ho! Ho! Ho!'.

It's unlikely that there will be any reciprocal gestures from those responsible for that other favourite Christmas scene, the Crib. It might be tempting to raise standards there too. The baby really should have a proper crib, not an animals' feeding trough. The walls should be draught proof. The family should have its own space, not be cheek by jowl with cows and goats.

But to tidy up that scene would be to take away its meaning. Jesus was born into a chaotic, confused world. The point of the Crib is to remind us that when God chose to come and be part of our lives, he did so in a manner that showed us he didn't expect VIP treatment. He came to be part of human experience at its toughest and most demanding.

Few of us have lives which go to plan and leave us untroubled. The fact that Jesus experienced the same kind of messiness and struggle as we do, gives us confidence that when we seek God's support in dealing with our troubles, he knows what we're on about. Tidying it all up is not usually what he does, but the Crib guarantees that he will be with us in our confusion and help us through it.

Read For because he himself has suffered and been tempted, he is able to help those who are tempted. *(Hebrews 2:18)*

Rejoice that God embraced the challenge of being human.

Reflect When am I aware of having experienced God's support?

Remember that God is backing me up even when I'm not conscious of it.

Resolve to try living with, not struggling against, the bits of my life which feel chaotic or messy.

Saturday

Walking fully grown tigers on a leash is all part of a day's work for a group of Buddhist monks in Thailand. They take in tigers which have been injured but not killed, sometimes by hunters and sometimes by people who didn't want the tiger near their village but also didn't want to see it die. 'We are a big family here,' said the head monk, sitting cross-legged on a rock surrounded by five large tigers who take turns to nuzzle up affectionately to their saffron-robed master.

The monks live with the possibility that an outburst of aggression and potentially destructive violence may occur suddenly and without warning. So do most of us. Hidden deep within most human beings is a well of frustration and anger. We become aware of it particularly when we feel provoked or threatened. It can seem powerful. Indeed, so strong does it sometimes feel, that we may worry that one day we'll be unable to control it.

The child born in the stable died on the Cross as a result of that violence. Throughout his life, he met it – in the violent behaviour ascribed to evil spirits, in the anger of his opponents, even in the misunderstanding of his disciples and his betrayal by one of them. But like the monks, he befriended those who expressed it. By coming into the world and living with gentleness alongside confused, destructive and aggressive people, he defused the power of their anger.

As we prepare to celebrate a festival of peace, let's be confident in what the Christmas story says about God coming into our violent world and overcoming its power. It can give us the courage to live at ease alongside any potential for violence or anger within ourselves and know that ultimately, there's a power that's stronger than it is.

Read Jesus met a man 'whom no one could bind any more . . . chains he wrenched apart, fetters he broke in pieces' but Jesus sent the unclean spirits into the pigs and the man found 'his right mind'. *(Mark 5:1–20)*

Rejoice that in the way he died and in his rising from death, Jesus defeated the forces that killed him.

Reflect What do I normally do with my anger?

Remember when I'm inwardly raging, God's arms hold me firmly and lovingly.

Resolve to befriend my anger, not criticise myself for it.

Week four

Coming

Fourth Sunday in Advent

When a statue of the baby Jesus was stolen from a nativity scene, the South Australian Brewing Company offered a reward for its return. They promised six cases of beer to anyone who returned the statue to the company's traditional nativity display. 'We are very concerned about the well-being of Baby Jesus and we are calling for his swift and safe return,' said SABC's managing director.

The one whose birth is the reason for the parties and fun at this time of year, is frequently absent from the minds of those enjoying them. Christmas without Christ is the experience of the majority in the western world. But Christ's exclusion from Christmas isn't entirely inappropriate. After all, the biblical story suggests that God chose to come into the world without a great deal of fuss and palaver. Mary and Joseph, themselves of no great social significance, would have hardly been likely to shout about the pregnancy for fear of being thought either immoral or mad. Only a few chosen people, themselves outsiders in that culture, were party to the significance of what was happening.

Perhaps God prefers a certain anonymity. When he does become the focus of attention, he is so frequently misrepresented. In the life of the world and in our own lives too, it's often what's going on underneath the surface and the changes which at first seem insignificant, that in the end have the most profound effect.

The South Australian Brewing Company may well be concerned about the well-being of their statue, but the absence of an often over-sentimentalised and insipid image of Christ from many Christmas celebrations, doesn't mean the real Jesus isn't there.

Read Mary said, 'My soul celebrates the Lord, and my spirit rejoices in God my Saviour, for he has looked with favour on the lowliness of his servant'.
(Luke 1:46–48)

Rejoice that God often chooses to become part of my life without me realising it.

Reflect Is anything happening in me beneath the surface where Christ might be at work?

Remember that God works effectively even when he's not the focus of attention.

Resolve to expect to find Jesus in unexpected places.

Monday

The ReadyWhenUR kettle is operated by text message. It contains a radio receiver and levers which turn the kettle on when an SMS message is picked up. Tea company PG Tips who have worked with Orange to produce the kettle are hoping for success. A spokesman said: 'It's a great gadget that will give people longer to see their favourite TV shows.'

Modern technology is making it easier to do all sorts of things from a distance. We can shop without going to shops, we can confer with colleagues all over the world without leaving the office, we can see our photographs without taking them to be developed. It is becoming distinctly unfashionable to have to make the effort to go anywhere.

God's choice to come into our world shows that God was prepared to 'make an effort'. He'd had enough of doing things from a distance and wanted to come and share in what it is to be human, with all its joys and its struggles. The result was that he experienced the same challenge as we do to respond to his fellow human beings' needs. The real world isn't one where people sit in their armchairs enjoying every modern convenience, but a world where there are many demands on anyone who is prepared to go out of their way to bring support, comfort and healing to others.

There is lots to be grateful for in contemporary labour-saving devices. But God has set us an example of the kind of committed caring which is not labour-saving at all, but involves the giving of time and energy. We can follow his example most effectively when in doing so we seek the help of the one who set it.

Read Let the same mind be in you which was in Christ Jesus who . . . emptied himself taking the form of a slave. *(Philippians 2:5, 7)*

Rejoice that God perseveres when I make it hard for him to love me.

Reflect How might I put more effort into my relationship with Christ?

Remember sometimes it's caring for myself I need to put more effort into.

Resolve to go out of my way to care for some-one.

Tuesday

After Babs the gorilla died at age 30, keepers at Brookfield Zoo in the States, decided to allow surviving gorillas to mourn her. Babs' nine-year-old daughter, Bana, was the first to approach the body. She sat down, held Babs' hand and stroked her mother's stomach. Then she laid her head on Babs' arm. Other gorillas approached Babs and gently sniffed the body. Koola, brought her infant daughter and held her close to Babs, as she had frequently done when Babs was alive. 'I had a headache for the rest of the day after all the tears I cried watching them,' said their keeper.

Touching was central to the way these gorillas expressed their grief. There are many other emotions touching can convey. Comfort, affection, reassurance, sympathy as well as greeting and farewell can all be physically expressed. One of the messages of Christmas is that God wanted to be able to express feelings in physical ways. By being born in the flesh, God not only made bodily contact with the world. God also experienced something new – the delight that having a body with all its sensations can bring.

Jesus knew the value of touch – he often touched those he was healing – and God's coming to touch the world with his presence was partly to offer us healing. There's a power in touch that words or actions alone can't match. Using our hands and bodies to communicate with those we care for, to share with them how we're feeling and to offer them tenderness, is a gift God's given us too.

Read Jesus took her by the hand and said, 'My child . . .' *(Luke 8:54)*

Rejoice in the delight that touch can bring.

Reflect Would I benefit from asking someone close to me for more touching or hugs?

Remember that God's touch in my life can heal me.

Resolve to use touch today to offer someone comfort or encouragement (remembering that some people's past experience makes being touched unwelcome).

Wednesday

One of the exhibits in the National Toy Hall of Fame at the Strong Museum in Oregon is a cardboard box. 'Low-tech and unpretentious it may be, but the cardboard box has fostered learning and creativity for multiple generations and in many cultures,' said the chief curator. 'I think every adult has had that disillusioning experience of picking what they think is a wonderful toy for a child and then finding the kid playing with the box. It's that empty box full of possibilities that the kids can sense and the adults don't always see.'

There are enormous possibilities for fun in the simplest and most unlikely things. It often takes a childlike attitude to see them, but it's an attitude people of any age can develop. Something similar is true of the ability to become aware of God. Children are fascinated by boxes because their imagination enables them to see more than is actually there. It becomes a spaceship, castle or a haven to daydream in. Discovering God in our lives is not 'imagining things' but the process is helped by having imagination. There are places and times where most people expect to be conscious of God because of their religious connotations, but a playful attitude to life is often helpful in finding him in less obvious places – not least because there's something playful in God too.

Developing the capacity to have fun will enrich us. It might also help us become more open to letting God come to us in the simple, ordinary aspects of our lives.

Read Wisdom was at [God's] side each day, his darling and delight, playing in his presence continually, playing over his whole world. *(Proverbs 8:30–31)*

Rejoice in the fun I have.

Reflect Are there any ways in which I take myself too seriously?

Remember with God I am safe enough to let my seriousness go.

Resolve to 'become like a child'. *(Mark 10:15)*

Thursday

Dog lovers in Japan can now get to see the world as their pets do. Toy maker, Tomy, has launched a tiny digital camera which can be attached to the dog's collar. It can take pictures by using a remote control, letting owners 'enjoy pictures from their dogs' view,' the company said. Or owners can put on a time switch taking pictures at intervals of one minute to one hour.

The capacity to understand how things look from someone else's point of view is a gift. But it is one we can develop as a way of enlarging our ability to offer appropriate care and sensitive support. It also adds richness to our lives when we're able to enjoy, not only our own way of seeing things, but can also get glimpses of other people's too.

The Bible's understanding of what happened in the birth of Jesus is, among other things, that God got to see what human life is like from the inside. This is reassuring for us because we can know that when we seek God's help, the one we are approaching for support and care, knows what it's like to be human. But it seems it was important for God too – taking flesh expanded, so to speak, God's experience – and God clearly saw the process as a vital aspect of his love for the world.

The cameras used by dog owners only enable them to see what their dog sees – they're given no idea what the dog feels about it. If we try to get inside other people's skin as God got inside ours, we can at least begin to understand what makes them tick.

Read The home of God is among mortals. He will dwell with them. *(Revelation 21:3)*

Rejoice that God is intimately aware of how I'm feeling.

Reflect Is there anyone whose motivation or internal dynamics I need to work harder to understand?

Remember empathy is very difficult when my experience of life is very different from the other person's – but it's worth trying.

Resolve to see something from someone else's point of view today.

Friday

One Christmas, Madame Tussauds ruffled feathers by displaying a nativity scene in which Hugh Grant and Graham Norton were among the shepherds, Tony Blair, the Duke of Edinburgh and George Bush were wise men and Joseph and Mary were represented by David and Victoria Beckham. The characters were chosen by public vote.

The tableau may not have been in good taste, but more importantly it ignored a central theme in the Christian celebration of Christmas. The characters in the biblical story are all unknowns. Even the place where the baby was born – Bethlehem – was 'least of all the cities of Judah' until it was chosen as Christ's birthplace.

No public vote would have produced the same result as God's choice. God wanted to challenge human judgements about status and to make clear how important and valuable apparently insignificant people are.

There are millions of people all over the world whose status, measured in economic or social terms, is insignificant. Their plight must often seem to them to have been forgotten by those of us who are in a position to do something to bring them greater justice. Nearer to home too, there'll be people we know who're feeling sidelined or unimportant.

'We're sorry if we have offended people,' said a spokeswoman for the museum. She said they had tried to respect tradition, using a plastic doll in the manger. It's no plastic doll, but a real baby, who shares in the experience of millions in our world who know what it's like to be forgotten and anonymous.

Read He has brought down the powerful from their thrones and lifted up the lowly. *(Luke 1:52)*

Rejoice that people don't have to be important to matter to God.

Reflect How affected am I by people's status?

Remember when I recognise someone's innate value, I'm contributing to their well-being, especially when I let them know it.

Resolve to look for an opportunity to affirm someone who might be feeling unnoticed.

Christmas Eve

'2B? NT2B?=???' is a text message version of Hamlet's famous soliloquy. Dot Mobile, a company offering mobile phones to students, has hired a professor of English Literature to offer subscribers text message summaries of literary classics and quotations from them. The climax of *Romeo and Juliet* is that 'bothLuvrs kill Emselves,' while Jane Austen's *Pride and Prejudice* concludes when 'Evry1GtsMaryd.'

Such summaries may well convey factual information about what happens in these well-known works of literature. But they don't capture their full emotional force. For this you need proper words.

When the fourth Gospel describes Jesus as the Word, its writer was perhaps recognizing a similar truth. Every previous experience of God had been a summary compared with the truth and wonder of his coming in the flesh. The Hebrew experience of God had been varied, often very personal and almost always powerful. Yet those who knew Jesus felt that everything that came before was only a pale reflection of the God now fully revealed in him.

The truth of what we celebrate tomorrow is almost impossible to put into words. It's a day when we remember that even God recognised their inadequacy and decided that his presence among us would say more effectively what needed to be said. Words remain enormously valuable as a way of communicating but as far as our understanding of God is concerned, we'd be a great deal worse off if the Word had never become flesh.

Read The Word became flesh and lived among us . . . full of grace and truth. *(John 1:14)*

Rejoice that God chose to give us his whole self.

Reflect Do my words always accurately reflect who I am?

Remember as with God's expressing of himself, so with mine: actions speak louder than words.

Resolve to look for an opportunity which feels safe to reveal a bit more of myself to someone I love.

Christmas Day

It took less than 10 minutes for Kubwa the elephant to deliver her 200-pound baby boy. But, though a month early, it had been 21 months since staff at Indianapolis Zoo had artificially inseminated her. 'Many elephants take days to deliver their offspring,' said a Zoo spokeswoman. 'He's just adorable. There's nothing like a baby elephant.'

Staff waiting for the great day were taken aback at how quickly it was all over. 'But now our part begins,' said the spokeswoman. The calf quickly learned to stand on a step stool to reach his unusually tall mother's udders and Kubwa formed an immediate strong bond with the baby. But the attentiveness and care of the zoo keepers was also crucial in those early days of the elephant's potential lifespan of 50–60 years.

The coming of Jesus was over in a flash when compared with the centuries God had used to prepare people for the moment. But the coming of the baby was not the end of the story. Continuing attentiveness and care from people like us is needed, if the potential let loose in that stable for a better world is to be realised.

What we celebrate today was a pivotal point in the life of the world. God offers us partnership in the task of creating a world of peace and justice for everyone. His coming to us initiates a momentum which each Christmas is a chance to re-establish. Let's hope today that that crucial moment in the stable is one which, increasingly, we and all people respond to. Working closely with God, there's no knowing where, through many years and over centuries, it might lead.

Read When the time had fully come, God sent his Son. *(Galatians 4:4)*

Rejoice in the inspiration that Christ's birth has been over two millennia.

Reflect What can I do to make a reality the 'peace on earth' of which the angels sang?

Remember that God's been working in the world since time began and will continue to do so.

Resolve to take seriously today and every day, God's presence in the world and in my life.